T0153167

Trace

Also by Eric Pankey

Eric Pankey

Trace

Poems

milkweed
editions

© 2013, Text by Eric Pankey
All rights reserved. Except for brief quotations in critical articles or reviews, no part of this book may be reproduced in any manner without prior written permission from the publisher: Milkweed Editions, 1011 Washington Avenue South, Suite 300, Minneapolis, Minnesota 55415. (800) 520-6455
www.milkweed.org

Published 2013 by Milkweed Editions
Printed in Canada
Cover design by Rebecca Lown Design
Cover art © 2012 by Susan Rothenberg / Artists Rights Society (ARS), New York
Author photo by Rachel Eliza Griffiths
Interior design by Hopkins/Baumann
The text of this book is set in Adobe Caslon Pro.
13 14 15 16 17   5 4 3 2 1
First Edition

Please turn to the back of this book for a list of the sustaining funders of Milkweed Editions.

Library of Congress Cataloging-in-Publication Data

Pankey, Eric, 1959-
    Trace : poems / Eric Pankey. -- 1st ed.
        p. cm.
    ISBN 978-1-57131-449-9 (acid-free paper)
    I. Title.
    PS3566.A575T73 2013
    811'.54--DC23

                                        2012028097

This book is printed on acid-free paper.

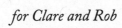

for Clare and Rob

Contents

III.

There ain't no dark till something shines
— Townes Van Zandt

Trace

I.

The Sacrifice

Gradually, the blood drains:
A thousand words never meant for scripture.

Still hunkered on the mountain ridge,
The moon: a saline ghost, a mouth

Opened around a hollow syllable.
When we move toward the sacrifice,

God lifts as a swarm — a body of flies —
As sated as God ever is.

A Bird Loose in the House

The frame — a grid — contrives a theater,
A shadow-play alive on a curtain alive with wind.

Call the bird
The arbitrary inventoried in its variety,

Or perhaps
The embarkation into the ongoingness that follows.

The grid — at once minimal and complex —
Holds curves and intersections,
                                        the plot
And the plotted, point by point,
Its line, its echoic spiraling.

Call the bird
The breath that blossoms and wilts.

Displaced, the bird afflicts the space,
Is the stigma by which the flawless is affirmed.

Call the bird
A sparrow

Call the house
The house we live in,
The house of the Lord forever.

The Place of Skulls

One crow, perched on the gallows, oversees the folly.
Still daylight — long shadows of a low sun —
The visible hides the visible.

Somewhere constellations turn like millstones.
After the body's hauled down, the tree resumes
Its life as a tree: blossoming in season, bearing fruit.

Prayer

When you left it was as if a glacier retreated,
As if the ice tonnage, which rasped, scraped, and scoured for ages,
Diminished in a moon's single phase to a trickle of meltwater.

I live in its aftermath — till, eskers, erratics, cirques, exposed bedrock.

Moss darkens the far side of a granite boulder. Pines.
Then the valley fills with hardwood forest, which burns and grows again,
Which burns and grows again, which burns and grows again.

Edge of Things

I wait at the twilit edge of things,
A dry spell spilling over into drought,

The slippages of shadow silting in,
The interchange of dusk to duskier,
The half-dark turning half-again as dark.

There: night enough to call it a good night.

I wait for the resurrection, but wake to morning:
Mist lifting off the river.
Ladders in the orchard trees although the picking's done.

The Calling of the Elect to Heaven

Next to where nettles grow in the vacant lot,
Drawers, left open and empty in a dresser,
Warp, half-filled with rain. The low sky is ashen.
Although workers climbed down years ago, a grid
Of poles and planks still scaffolds the church steeple.
No one pulls the rope slumped over its pulley.
No one can recall the last hour sounded.
My breath, as I lean close, darkens the window.
Only nails on the walls where pictures once hung.

Ritual

Each year, a garland-crowned goat is driven into the wilderness.
Repetition is an aid to memory.

A garland-crowned goat, driven into the wilderness,
Takes with it the burden of its sacrifice.

Each year we drive out the garland-crowned goat.
The goat makes a last meal of its crown.

The Truth of Scripture

Sunlight dapples on a horse's flank.
                                A virga
Hangs in the vast western sky like Heaven's gate.

A virga hangs in the sky like an embrasure.

Little by little the porch empties of light
And one reads until each turned page is a blank.

Night, parenthetical, is not the subject.

One reads until each page is blank,
                                keeps reading,
As if the truth of scripture will be revealed.

Night — an unstable, volatile amalgam —
Gives way to day and words emerge from the page,

As opaque as ever, riddling, random.
One looks up and the horse is gone.
                                What transport

It offered, now absent.
So one returns to the page, studies what's there.

The Creation of Adam

A lizard circled the marble lip of the wellhead.
In the wind, a shutter banged, disturbed the sparrow flock,
Which lifted like a sail, only to settle again on cobbles.

The other noon sounds? A horse turning a millstone.
Rust inching up a drainpipe. The spilling of sand
Down an anthill. The dog whimpering in a dream.

Bees shuttled between the hive and the garden.
On a cross of branches tied with baling wire,
An old man hung a ragged wool overcoat.

As he weeded, he instructed the scarecrow
On the doctrine and conundrum of free will.
When a crow landed on the scarecrow's shoulder,

The scarecrow, who had listened well, knew
If he chose, he could shrug and shoo the crow.
If he chose. And could shrug. And could move his lips.

As of Yet

Call it paradise, this enclosure of trees.
No graves yet. No seasons. Time itself

As of yet uncreated. Nothing as of yet
Handmade. No stone knife. No bone needle.

No spear point. Call it paradise
Where a flint has yet to spark or deadfall

Flare beneath lightning, flare, then
Smother in a downpour, the char

Slick black beneath a first rainbow.
He has yet to learn to slaughter or tame the wolf,

To don the wolf-mask. As of yet, her body
Has not opened into birth, pain, and burden.

Beyond the enclosure of trees, a scattering
Of rocks they must still name and knap into tools:

Chert, agate, chalcedony, and for miles —
Quick-quenched lava: *obsidian.*

Works and Days

At the fray of memory

A drop of sweat down her breast veers and misses her nipple

Chaos, it's said, was born first

Riverside willow leaf turns, turns, caught in an eddy

Instant yet everlasting

Iron oxide, smeared ochres, charcoal gestures: flanks, tusks, hooves

Cuckoo song among the oaks

Orion at the horizon; linens freeze on a line

By noon shade evaporates

At the fray, at the fray of memory

Primitive Water

Cherry blossoms on the ink-stone —

Gutters, leaf-choked, overflow —

The path along the ridgeback washed out —

Seedlings, saplings, a poplar girded with wrist-thick vines —

If not for the gnarled, knuckley habit of words I might at last have
a purchase on silence —

The deer freeze, skitter, then fly —

Snare of antlers —

The burden and effort of constructing meaning —

The quick bickering of jays —

The river seen from above as the character for *dragon* —

Five crows roost and shake down blossoms —

Myth, not history, predates one's childhood —

There one can disinter the gibbous moon, the essential Arcanum,
the primitive water's source —

Models of Paradise

The mountain, all haze and mist,
Is without fixed form,
                        yet by mid-morning
It stands clear: an ax-trimmed jade fragment.

::

After the afterimage slips away,
One utters against
                the utter silence
And time congeals again, as always, as matter.

::

The water tastes of lead, or rather the aftertaste of lead:
Honey of exile,
            salt of *lacrimae antiquae* —
One part per billion yet distinct.

::

Distracted, I looked around as others prayed.
Sinew fitted to bone.
                              Muscle to sinew.
The body's dust is dust.

                    : :

Ice, a cold weld, holds for now.
A translation of silence
                              is silence.
Swallows flicker at the fog-edge.

                    : :

As lightning roots, it withers.
Sometimes I exist
                    only as anxiety —
Flamelike, a shifting, ambiguous shape.

                    : :

The dark displaces, gram by gram,
The weightless light.
                    Within each moment,
A New Jerusalem, an Eden outside history.

                : :

One must penetrate the invisible to reside in the visible.
The body is always
                    a trope in these arguments,
A terse balance between gnosis and muscle memory.

                : :

As events unfold, the fog skulks,
Blots out what was mountain
                        (or *is* mountain)
With a gray continuity beyond the margins.

                : :

Sleet returns to its quarry.
Through the boreal dusk:
                              a sparrow-flash.
Night is a loose thread pulled from a sampler.

                    : :

No angel. No flaming sword.
Just stars above me,
                    a broken abacus of stars:
The beads scattered, the beads unthumbed.

                    : :

Lit as if from beneath by the drowned moon's
Camphor,
                    the current's silver quickens.
Eddies uncoil behind an oar blade.

                    : :

Ten thousand galaxies strung among the stag's antlers
Stand in as variorum,
                    evidence
Already obsolete, and thus, evocative.

                    : :

The mass graves were left unexcavated.
So that ships might sail to Troy,
                         an offering.
The unnamed dead remain unnamed.

                    : :

Roots in air, figs gathered from thistle,
Sky-writing,
              web-shadow, solvents . . .
What we lack, mostly, is context.

                    : :

22 The stray dog returns as an oracle
With ears and tail down,
                              shadow detached.
Doesn't look like good news after all.

                    : :

Spirits abandon their abode, don masks.
Each mask
          tells its own story.
The mask, not the wearer, tells its own story.

                    : :

If I allow myself, I can taste
It all in the honey:
                    tupelo, tiger lily,
An extinct thistle from Tangiers . . .

                    : :

Unseen, the osprey calls within the fog.
In all directions,
                    the same day starts.
One measures the void a gram at a time.

: :

Ghosts jostle one another at the ditch
Filled with blood.
                    They cannot speak unless bribed.
So we fill up the ditch and watch them flock.

: :

If the world is a mere seeming,
Why does so much dust
                    gather on the baseboard?
Even in my emptying mind: dust.

: :

Toadflax, creeping buttercup, shepherd's purse;
A skirmish of birds;
               the dividual;
The inexhaustible light of childhood.

           : :

On display like an écorché's flayed flesh,
Every memory,
              mediated by scars,
May as well be a signed deposition.

           : :

I had a vision of the hereafter.
No flame or gnashing.
               Just a table set
With bread and milk, a large knife, cups for all.

           : :

We bundled wheat together, called it our god.
The roof we lived beneath,
                                merely a translation
Of the word *roof,* kept out no rain.

                     : :

Foretold by an entourage of dragonflies,
The fox entered
                     and tossed the vole's bones:
The random arrayed to reveal a model of paradise.

                     : :

Here we say, meaning a locus, a lesion.
Here we say
                     (although the days scud by)
And in saying so render the space more empty.

II.

The Burning House

The roof, a hand-drawn triangle, burned
With a clear, soundless, unconsuming fire,

Like desire untinged by violence or object,
Burned all night in a dream, bright like light

Dissolved from gold, and wan and drawn
Like orpiment thinned with gall-tempered wine,

The house afire, the house of my childhood,
All tinder and kindling married to spark,

Burned, the flames neither transmuting nor decaying,
Flicking forth, the child's drawing of a house

Stands: a door, two windows, the fire locked inside.

Moon Phases Carved on a Bone

One can interrogate the stars,
Count the barbs as they slope
Toward the feather's tip,

Make of prime numbers
A hive of the mind,
Speculate with images.

At the shore of waking,
A fragment insinuates narrative,
A sequence of events, phases:

The half-moon adorned in its cornhusk mask,
The crescent moon as it sheds
Scree, grit, pollen, and spores,

The straw effigy of the new moon —
Expiatory, a jabber of smoke —
Rendered, reduced to a notion.

Yet awake, one recalls mere sleep,
Not the torch-marks on the bear's skull,
Not the blister the burin rubbed up.

Southern Elegy

As shadows skew to the east
A garter snake lifts its head,
Catches the moment's scent

And freezes there, then lowers its head
And moves on along cracked masonry
Marked by rust, along slate

Slabs in the unkempt graveyard.
Sometimes I can foresee the future
Between the loose weft of hours,

But mostly I live here in the capricious present
Writing down one thing, then the next.
Autumn passes like empty freight cars —

Some doors open, some doors closed —
Light flickers and flashes through the cracks.
The trees are a thousand species of fire.

Cogitatio Mortis

Although I forage for words to shape thought,
I long to be voiceless, outside hours.

Hard to remember when the gods last intervened.
The fleeing lovers transformed into gazelles?
The levee built a foot higher than the crest?

Beyond a field blind in shadow,
A crow — standoffish — chuckles.

::

I could go on like this: list after list,
A compendium meant to do nothing
More than to place me here:

Pointing north, bewitched like a compass needle.

Hard to make much that resembles poetry
Out of one's depression, which is mute, lethargic,
Leaden — articulate only as *stalled-ness,* as *stilled-ness.*

After the problem's solved, there's still the proof to slog through.

::

In the underworld, with a seed placed under my tongue,
I make conversation solely from questions
And answers in a foreign phrase book.

I speak and watch my words warp — veil
And unveil — their objects. *Is the post office open?*

No, it is closed on Sundays. Is it always this cold?
No, it is usually quite balmy this time of year.

All of winter, like a suppressed yawn, wells up inside me.

         : :

Dunes shift, diminish; shift and stay.

I set out as one sets a fire, fire being its own motive.
I walk and a minute strays into an hour,
The hours into algorithms of chance.

The tidal creek runs fast: a cut length of silk
Still dry the moment before it sinks.

The shapeless water shapes the coast.
A tanker, at the horizon, slips into an amalgam of murk.

         : :

Once, I chipped from rock a fossilized fern,

A limestone relief from where in shaded crevices
Ferns still grew. How as a boy did I affix memory
Before I had words to tether it?

Cousin to thunder, the crow foretold a change in weather.

When I drew a pictograph with limestone onto shale,
It possessed no ritual meaning: the image of *snake*
Read as *snake* — until a thunderstorm washed it away.

: :

I may as well be a ghost, burdened by gravity,
A sleet-heavy rag-heap on the road's shoulder.

In each object, a narrative hibernates:
Shark's tooth, shark's eye, mermaid's purse,
Glut of guts the seagulls feed on.

I wake entangled in the threadbare riggings

And imagine the clutter and mess
Before the creation of the maggot and the microbe.

: :

Above: the forgotten vignettes of constellations.
On the river, the ache-song of a slow thaw;
Each stone, anchored, measures the same hour.

I hitched home, which means I walked most of the way.

After awhile, the journey is thread spun from distance and sleet.
Moon on the pond like an open door.
After awhile, each room is a waiting room.

        : :

The crow dallies on a waist-high stump.
Not a thought but the things before me.
Where water flooded three days ago

A loose script of debris, gully beds
Gravelly, clay-dank. And as evening
Commences: a firefly. Here. No, there:

The far bank chafed with slow water.
Unhurried, yet headlong, night falls
With its continuums and fluxes,

Shadows recede and billow, suspended
Not solvent, in the encompassing, discernable dark.

Out-of-the-Body

This morning I watch a river otter and wonder
If it is at play or work, or if for the otter
There is no distinction. Below the falls, it scrambles
Onto border ice, slips into the quick current,
Submerges, pulled downstream, then reemerges, steaming,
Onto a breakup jam, and clambers back to the falls
And begins again.
                      Out-of-the-body, one is lonely
In ecstasy, and that is why such moments are rare,
Because there is only so much loneliness a heart
Can filter in a given life and then must give out.
Some nights, I find myself alive beside you, awake
For an instant, and then asleep. Awake for an instant
Then asleep, beside you. Moonlight, twenty years ago.
Moonlight fell on the sheets, on your breasts still full of milk.

The Repeated Image

Gray dawn, gray dusk, the day between:
An adagio, tones diminished by space and time — slow, exhausting.

Underfoot, the orchard ground is soft, pungent with rot.
The barn owl, grammarian of weather and plagues, wakes to a throng
        of crows.

Don't be naïve, a neighbor scolds,
Sometimes brutality must be met with brutality.

Gray dusk, gray dawn, the night between: parenthetical.
I hold her thighs lightly with both hands, with my tongue, unfold
        the folded.

Autumn slipped by unnoticed: a poem written —
Concealed and smuggled — on the back of a sutra.

We got so tired of watching the war on TV:
The same body dragged through the street,

Snagged for a moment in a pothole,
Snagged but kicked free by a boy.

The low moon, unearthed, burns with alcohol's cold blue flame.
She says, *Come up from there and kiss me.*

A Stone to Place on a Cairn

Time is its own ransom.

The rain stops momentarily to mark a comma
Between one Ice Age and the next:

A palm-stone, a sling-stone,

A pocket-stone, a stone
To place on a cairn.

To disambiguate the present tense,

I read crow entrails displayed
(A loose knot, an ampersand)

Holding together that which falls apart:

The *once* and the *to be,*
The frost-gnawed grain.

Iron, rusting, grows inward.

The nettle — ruderal, tenuous —
Anchors in the gravel pit.

The overwrought amaryllis

And the peony's heady head
Are vermillions (from sulfur

And mercury sublimed)

And only in memory:
Each now out of season.

The caged chameleon is fluent in *green.*

Archaic Reverie

Dragonfly shadow jostles
The shallow stream's still surface.

Not a breeze, but higher up
Something shepherds the storm clouds west.

Bees make wax for saints' candles,
Honey to sweeten the grain.

Overflowing with water
A wood pail thuds the well-wall.

Listen to the cicada:
The whetted edge of its song,

These months before straw girds sheaves,
Before the wind-lifted chaff

Swirls off the threshing floor.

Trace

Flushed and scattered quail
Resolve as a genus of randomness.

Antlers hold open the sky.

Ground porphyry, slaked lime,
And mineral spirits set down
Mimic the dun-hazed hills.

To depict, one dissects, distorts,
Preserves, or adumbrates.

One mars surfaces, makes of ground
A figure, of a figure a ground.

Where to place the horizon line
On the picture plane,
                              or how
To enunciate the heat-warped air,
To suggest the lake's analog,
Or twilight's paltry allotment?

To occupy a space is to shape it.

Snow, slantwise, is not white
But a murk of winter-black basalt.

In the gullied, alluvial distances,
On the swallow-scored air,

Each erasure is a new trace.

Objects and Mementos

In a room above, an unseen canary ceases its song;
Moisture condenses and clings, clouds

The glass of a stoppered antique bottle;
An onion, fallen behind the cupboard, sprouts.

Objects and mementos are not memory,
But vessels of, frames for.

To strike the noon hour,
The lightning rods flare all at once.

The shutters are nailed open.
The story, within, there to be read.

In the wine tannins, I taste the sun.
I see the thermals by way of the up-spiraling hawk.

A Line Made by Walking

Below: a ravine green with fern.
        And deeper still, a moss-edged sinkhole.

Nothing, it seems, but a crescent moon all April,
A mute yoke with which to bear a burden.

Strewn across the high valley:
          stone-flakes, arrowheads, and
    the remains of ancient fires.
I long for nothingness, yet my flawed heart cannot keep up.

Above a terrace of fog-traces,
         water pools before the falls, then falls.

What day is not a feast day?
        I close my eyes and the image persists:
The glint of an unnamed hour. The path groomed by use.

A well calls forth sleeping waters.

Later, I'll look up and see a sky executed in silver-leaf,
Stars like a summer's catch afloat on a stringer.
           Or it's overcast,
Clouds like laden galleons moving like the past off to the left
    as I read toward the *now*.

The mockingbird,
          fluent in every tongue but its own,
Tries out the song plankton makes as it filters sunlight.

Every thing, Paul Eluard says, *can be compared to everything.*
                             Every thing finds its echo,
Its reason, its resemblance, its contrast, its becoming, everywhere.

The storm still far off,
                    yet two or three drops fall
Like dabs of sealing wax upon the table.

          : :

Clouds pile up, then part. From the pines, dew drips.
Behind smoke haze: the worn-down Blue Ridge.

If the world is but a veil,
                    why this cold at my bones, this fever in which I
        am swaddled?

I am not myself tonight, I say, meaning: *that is all I am.*

One of the trucks hauling away the town's dismantled carnival runs
        over a skunk.
I catch on the wind a whiff of my own past:
                        an acrid, wiry thread of distance.

How obvious it seems now:
                            without expectation one feels less disappointment.

As always, the future is just ahead:
A badly tuned car idling on the gravel shoulder.

After the storm, chain saws harass the afternoon. Bees weigh down
        the lavender.

Take heart, I console myself:
Days arrive, one at a time, more than a little unkempt.

Is that the wind in the grass or the shimmer of a startled snake?
If I could graph a curve or chart the meanders
                            or pinpoint the instant of dissolution,

I might transcribe the severe elegance of the sun just up.
The day-moon is jade: milky, vitreous dream-larva.

A hawk circles the fallow-lands.
                        Barbwire darkens with rust.

The rest of the day waits beyond the rutted path like an almshouse.

                    : :

The dog finds a fox skull in a fern-bank,
                            paws at it;
Picks up deer scent; nose down, moves on.

I follow, the leash taut, go where I'm pulled.
Autumn dusk: creek after rain,
                    silt-heavy, swollen, rapid over submerged rocks.

Deer tracks end at a thicket, but the dog continues to tug.

Let's head home, I say. The leash goes slack and he follows me.

Memory like a black hole distorts time.
Snow on the windfall.
                    Cusp of ice where a hoof sank in mud.

If all matter is constant, what can one add to creation?

Not bitter, but thaw-cold.
                    Except when the winds blow.
As I walk, I live inside my thoughts, a dwelling all cellar and attic.

If I track what leaves no trace, why does each outing circle back home?

Uphill, a fox bark.
                    Smoke hangs slack above chimneys.
Low winter sun on fallen pine needles.

A walk is never the theory of a walk,
                    or rather never merely.

The worked edge of the evening sky
Is what I found as I looked for a place to hide.

It wouldn't be a long story if it could be made short.

The Passing Moment

One word, the smallest intervention —
Ax, say, or *owl,*
             the sharp fall and cleft
That each evokes — excavates a past.

As through a grammar that transposes
What one knows,
             one knows indirectly
And makes of absence its echo.

How to illumine the passing moment
(Archived as memory
          in memory)
Before one can say *now* or *you see?*

      It has rained or is about to.
      It has rained or is about to cease.

In the thicket, hung with yellow jackets,
Mottled shade, and gnats,
             sun glares
On the rained-on or about-to-be-rained-on blackberries.

The Last Word

Born of fire, the salamander, slowed by the cold calculus
Of the rain, bides its time.

The goldsmith hides his mark at the bristling heart
Of the bees' honeyed pavilion.

Cut, the Tree of Life (also known as a Dragon Tree)
Oozes red translucent sap.

When you enter the Underworld by way of cellar doors,
You should leave them open

Like a dictionary on a stand: the last word looked up
Marred by a thumb-smudge.

III.

Cold Mountain Meditations

Hidden behind the cloud-spill: cold mountain.
Outside time, the river runs as it has run: *tense-less*.

In the rapids and eddies: frazil ice, candled ice.

A trail of smoke. The thousand miles home.
Night is sumptuous ink bled to the edges.

   : :

If, as Plato once argued, a thing is not seen
Because it is visible, but conversely

Visible because it is seen, I'll close my eyes.
I am ready to exchange this season for the next.

I'll close my eyes to the whole sweet mess of today.
Depressed, I look for an antecedent, a cause,

But find instead fatigue and its permutations.
By stint of flinty light, I'll look away.

   : :

I try to fix the moment, but it unknots and slips.

I try to fathom the scale of grays between this river
And the light years, as yet unstarred, reflected there.

   : :

How does one align the field notes,
Or read the specter of narrative
When even the light is lethargic, leaden?

So little is legible: glacial till,
Moonlight on the iced-over ditch,
The moon itself — a flint-edged pruning hook.

: :

If you see me, I'm the one dressed in shadow.

I move as a fever moves — a chill at first,
A meager ember passed from hand to mouth.

All winter I pace from one corner of the room
To the next: tentative in tenuous balance,

Singular and plural like dust, like snow.

: :

Where the crow walks: cuneiforms in the snow.
Light, turbulent light, coaxed up out of the depth,

(Where water flashes, falls, beside the red mill)

Regathers as broken ice in the backwash.
For the crow, *as-the-crow-flies* is no shortcut.

: :

The wall, crumbling, separates one muddy field from another,
Each a bog of thaw and milky ice, useless, yet still the wall

Defines the space, suggests a willful purpose and function
Worth the weight and haul, the previous mendings, the spine of it.

In this light: a narrow spectrum of earth tones — grays chalk-tinctured,
Reds of rust and raw ochre. Three birches, merely silhouettes,

Are moored to their shadows. Although a landscape can be rendered
As a repository of memory, I come empty

And empty-handed, remembering nothing of *the-once-before*.
No mortar, but gravel and grit level the field stones.

                    : :

Hawk on a dead snag. On the mountain, thunder.

No god offered us fire. A burning branch
Fell from a tree and we dragged it back home.

                    : :

Last night the shadows were ash-edged
As the moon moved behind clouds.

When I tried to ascend on the rungs of memory,
I found I had only a stepladder

And a rickety one at that,
So I returned to my house furnished with books.

The Book of Maladies and *The Book of Cures*
Shelved in separate rooms so as not to make things easy.

:   :

All shadows incline toward light.

The quarry pond, a diary without incident,
Offers mere surface: stagnant, flat gray.

Wind frets and lingers, lingers and frets.

One hour and then the next silts in.
Distance leads to an edge, a limit,

A slumped chimney in need of tuck-pointing

Or taking down. At noon, all is glare,
The clean and calcified air of an ossuary.

:   :

Like everyone else, I am waiting for death to intervene.
Until then I cobble hours into days. The sleet-swept birches darken.
There, in the sky's far corner, a star foretells its own cold collapse.

And then it is morning again: ice on the moss like old lace.
My mind opens and closes on the hinge of an afterthought.
Born out of emptiness, we return to the luxury of emptiness.

         : :

I look out on the landscape and see an interior,
A wilderness out of which a word

Arises and is heightened, changed. Arises then dissolves.
Morning mist, soon to burn off, conceals, for now, a mountain.

The distilled, absent subject shimmers, empty of itself.
As a dream relinquishes into language, the body,

Too, fills with wakefulness, the certainty of things
Unsettled by their names, by being named: *breath-stutter,*

Thaw-ice loose in the rapids, the cold stone-felt, permanent.
The present tense, endured, passes, remains tense and present.

Bluffs Above the Missouri

Rain's ended, but the river still rises.

One or two clouds as postscript.
Stars like floor nails shiny from wear.

The narrative of a river is in how
It diverges over distance from a straight line.

I set out on a picaresque journey
But return here: bluffs above the Missouri,
Not one day or another,

But the past divided by the memory of the past, its quotient.

Once I got lost with the wind and its attendants.
Once a boat, half-dragged onto shore, rocked like a derelict cradle.
Once a coyote, stiff-eared, mouth open, blocked the path.

The Dead Go Down to the Stygian Waters

My father stands empty-handed, waits for my brother.
By the river he waits, impatiently. A flock tilts,
Spirals, unfurls, settles serried in a maple.

The water is volatile, shape-shifts from rain to mist,
To the river's sluggish tug, silk then tarnished silver.
The hawk, scholar of thermals, turns above the windbreak.

Frost crystals on the scat; rust pinpoints the wire's barb.
The dead go down to the Stygian waters, the dead
Go down. My father stands empty-handed. My brother —

Not late but on the other side — steps into the water
To ford the distance until he is in over his head
And to his surprise can breathe in this water as in air.

Waking Hungover in a Field, 1979

Beneath a thunderhead that darkens noon
A single white cloud
                dangles like a wasps' nest.

A tree stump — blunt mouth of smoke —
Smolders untended midfield.

What wind there is
                tightens like skin beneath a touch.
The white cloud, as rain begins to fall,

Turns as smooth and dark as a washing stone.

If one had not moved,
                I would not have seen
Beyond the tree line the other five deer.

Diptych with Fox and Hawk

A fox gleans mulberries;

Rain-dusk bleeds from the edges inward,
The rain, at last,
                    a wash of lamp-wick char.

If the world hates a thing too pure,
I've got no troubles.
                    Years ago, I walked

The old battlefield: found no bones, no ghosts,
Just the horizon's heat-bruised air,
                                    a mirage

With the substance of,
                    as substanceless as, a mirage.

            : :

Hawk-call, echo:
                    autumn eases into ice.

Solvent, hours loosen, dissolve.

How unlikely tomorrow:
                    a bridge
Of *and* and *and* and *and*

Held up by shallow-driven pilings.

Each word is belated.
                    A thing
Falls into ruin by its own weight.

The echo of echo hardly a hawk.

Throne of the Ancestors

If the dead return, they do so bodily:
Spirits imprisoned in matter like coals,
Ash-banked. Now, the rain frays, gives over to snow.

Twenty years since I looked out and saw him there:
My father, a ghost — a permeable blur,
Thin, unsheltered in an overcoat of sleet.

Tonight, no trace as I watch from the window.
When I cut down the pear tree, I left a stump.
If he returns, he can sit there, take his rest.

The House We Left Behind

The moon, kin to our bones,
Will not respond to our prayers:

Each word, now, a spendthrift ember.
The house we left behind

Is not shuttered or shut,
But occupied by other lives

Not so unlike our own.
How odd for us who lived there

And now must knock.
If the door opens

Perhaps only the wind will answer.
Perhaps we knock and those

Who come welcome us
For who we are: strangers.

Six Cast Hexagrams

The moon: a house built on a glacier.
The moon: swaddled like a foundling.

The angel opens her mouth and snow
(Not a single word)
                                is released.
Thoughts stray:
                        a noun meaning
That around which a trap closes.

: :

Night noises: a little tune
Composed only on the black keys.

The underworld sky,
                                measured in fathoms,
Purples at twilight but never grows dark.

As the battlefield ravens pick through the sacrifice,
I sharpen the plow-edge of words.

: :

The mountainside, clear cut,
Releases a mudslide, buries the sawmill.

The river chokes with scree and deadfall.
The hayloft remains empty.

Hard frost cannot arrest the plague.
Once upon the peaks:
                              cloud-fed waterfalls.

                    : :

To hold, in a dream,
A sparrow struggling to escape
Forebodes mischief.

Is it better to prefer the bite-mark of the chisel
To the mirror-surface of polished stone,
Rust's consummations to a writhe of smoke?

                    : :

64   The present moment is like two rooms —
Adjoining, identical —
                        one moves through in a dream.

Both are dark but vestigial light
Leaks beneath the doorframes.

In each room, the same painting:
A ship in a storm,
               the prow dipping beneath waves.

           : :

River-clouds. Rain on the river
Where the river doubles back,
                  but on all sides sun.

Memory, like fire,
           clings to its object.

In the gap of silence between bells,
In the moment after ecstasy
The self returns and fills in the blanks.

Anhedonia

I work all day moving dust around. 　　 In the husk and slough of memory:

A shoulder's slope, the curve of a breast;
A peony tumbled by rain;

The owl heard, not seen, at dusk and dawn . . .
No pleasure or pain in elegy,

Or Eros's half-erased canon,
Or the glum reconciliation

Between the *felt* and what one now *feels*.
Just what is the nominal subject?

My heart is like a window at night —
All reflection, nothing of the view.

And when I wake I can see only
The intricate hard frost-work etched there.

Distances

Despondent, I ponder the larkspur
But hear only rhyme:
                   ark, err, lurk, spar.

Far off: sluice-clatter on rocks,
A slipstitch of rapids and flash
Before the shallows.

I hear the wind speaking its riddles —
Each word snuffed before I can write it down.

The dark repose of distances,

The dark repose of distances
                               nicked by headlights:

Dark matter fills in the spaces.

Another day. Another chapter
In which the plot is postponed.
I made a wrong turn
                    and ended here.

My father said I'd come to nothing.
I do believe I have arrived.

Two horses, heads down,
                         consult the sweet grass.
Then one looks up as if to point the way.

To Dwell in Thought

There is no cure for this low-grade melancholy.
Like a snake, you are never far from your shadow.

Begin as if the reader knows the past,
Has forgotten as much as you have.

How stalled and earthbound the river —
Depths filled with cloud reflections,

Shallows solid where nothing blurs, nothing focuses.
Dusty light barely yields the objects it cloaks.

To dwell in thought is to live in the interregnum
And yet, on the other side of the river,

Chestnut, piebald, dapple-gray, and black roan
Slip over a hill toward a stable you have culled from memory.

For once, let the peony be a stand-in for *fullness*.
The peony, opening, spills yesterday's rain.

Sober Then Drunk Again

On the lightning-struck pin oak,
On the swayed spine of the Blue Ridge,
                              a little gold leaf.

Once I drank with a vengeance.
Now I drink in surrender.
The thaw cannot keep me from wintering in.

I prepare for death when I should prepare
For tomorrow and the day after
                         and the day after that.

A clinker of grief where once hung my heart.

Memory — moon-drawn, tidal.
The moon's celadon glaze dulls in the morning's cold kiln.

Acknowledgments

The author thanks the editors and staff of the following journals where these poems, or parts of them, many in earlier versions and with different titles, first found readers:

ABZ Press: "Moon Phases Carved on a Bone"
American Literary Review: "The Calling of the Elect to Heaven," "Six Cast Hexagrams"
The American Poetry Review: "The Sacrifice"
The Antioch Review: "The Dead Go Down to the Stygian Waters"
Cimarron Review: "The Place of Skulls"
The Cincinnati Review: "Sober Then Drunk Again"
Denver Quarterly: "The Burning House"
Field: "As of Yet," "The Creation of Adam," "Distances," "Edge of Things," "A Stone to Place on a Cairn"
Free Verse: "The Last Word"
The Gettysburg Review: "Out-of-the-Body," "The Passing Moment"
Green Mountains Review: "The House We Left Behind"
Image: "Prayer," "Cogitatio Mortis"
The Innisfree Poetry Journal: "Cogitatio Mortis"
The Iowa Review: "Models of Paradise"
Limp Wrist: "Throne of the Ancestors"
Literature and Belief: "Cold Mountain Meditations"
Margie: "The Repeated Image"
Natural Bridge: "Objects and Mementos"
New England Review: "Cogitatio Mortis," "To Dwell in Thought"
New Orleans Review: "Diptych with Fox and Hawk"
A Public Space: "A Bird Loose in the House"
Rooms Outlast Us: "Models of Paradise"
Salamander: "Ritual"
Talking River: "Southern Elegy," "The Truth of Scripture"
Witness: "Cold Mountain Meditations," "Trace"
The Yale Review: "Waking Hungover in a Field, 1979"

Several of the poems here were published in a chapbook, *Objects and Mementos*, by the Center for Book Arts in 2007. The chapbook was selected by Jane Hirshfield and Sharon Dolin and designed and hand printed by Barbara Henry.

Thanks to Gary Clark and the gracious community at the Vermont Studio Center in Johnson, Vermont, where a good number of these poems were begun. Thanks to the Sunday poetry group, members past and present, for their candid readings of early drafts of these poems. Thanks to the good people at Milkweed Editions for their generosity and their belief in the book and, in particular, to Wayne Miller for his keen editorial eye. As always, my gratitude and devotion to Jennifer Atkinson for her unwavering support and love.

Eric Pankey is the author of eight previous collections of poetry, most recently *The Pear as One Example: New and Selected Poems 1984–2008*. He is the recipient of the Walt Whitman Award, a Library of Virginia Poetry Prize, and fellowships from the National Endowment for the Arts, the John Simon Guggenheim Memorial Foundation, and the Ingram Merrill Foundation. His work has appeared in *The New Yorker, The Iowa Review, The Kenyon Review, Field, The Gettysburg Review,* and *Poetry Daily,* as well as numerous anthologies, including *The Best American Poetry* 2011 (edited by Kevin Young). He is currently Professor of English and Heritage Chair in Writing at George Mason University. He lives in Fairfax, Virginia.

More Poetry from Milkweed Editions

To order books or for more information,
contact Milkweed at (800) 520-6455
or visit our web site www.milkweed.org

Odessa
Patricia Kirkpatrick

The Fact of the Matter
Sally Keith

The Alphabet Not Unlike the World
Katrina Vandenberg

A Hotel Lobby at the Edge of the World
Adam Clay

Gaze
Christopher Howell

Milkweed Editions

Founded as a nonprofit organization in 1980, Milkweed Editions
is an independent publisher. Our mission is to identify, nurture
and publish transformative literature, and build an engaged
community around it.

Join Us

In addition to revenue generated by the sales of books we publish,
Milkweed Editions depends on the generosity of institutions
and individuals like you. In an increasingly consolidated and
bottom-line-driven publishing world, your support allows us to
select and publish books on the basis of their literary quality and
transformative potential. Please visit our Web site (milkweed.org)
or contact us at (800) 520-6455 to learn more.

Milkweed Editions, a nonprofit publisher, gratefully acknowledges sustaining support from the following:

Maurice and Sally Blanks
Emilie and Henry Buchwald
The Bush Foundation
The Patrick and Aimee Butler Foundation
Timothy and Tara Clark
Betsy and Edward Cussler
The Dougherty Family Foundation
Mary Lee Dayton
Julie B. DuBois
Joanne and John Gordon
Ellen Grace
William and Jeanne Grandy
Moira Grosbard
John and Andrea Gulla
Elizabeth Driscoll Hlavka and Edwin Hlavka
The Jerome Foundation
The Lerner Foundation
The Lindquist & Vennum Foundation
Sanders and Tasha Marvin
Robert E. and Vivian McDonald
The McKnight Foundation
Mid-Continent Engineering
The Minnesota State Arts
    Board, through an
    appropriation by the
    Minnesota State Legislature
    and a grant from the National
    Endowment for the Arts

Christine and John L. Morrison
Kelly Morrison and John Willoughby
The National Endowment for the Arts
Ann and Doug Ness
Jörg and Angie Pierach
The RBC Foundation USA
Deborah Reynolds
Cheryl Ryland
Schele and Philip Smith
The Target Foundation
Edward and Jenny Wahl

THE McKNIGHT FOUNDATION

ART WORKS.
arts.gov

CLEAN
WATER
LAND &
LEGACY
AMENDMENT

MINNESOTA
STATE ARTS BOARD

b BUSH
FOUNDATION

TARGET.

Interior design and typesetting
by Hopkins/Baumann
Printed on acid-free 100% postconsumer waste paper
by Friesens Corporation

ENVIRONMENTAL BENEFITS STATEMENT

Milkweed Editions saved the following resources by printing the pages of this book on chlorine free paper made with 100% post-consumer waste.

TREES	WATER	ENERGY	SOLID WASTE	GREENHOUSE GASES
3	**1,470**	**1**	**99**	**271**
FULLY GROWN	GALLONS	MILLION BTUs	POUNDS	POUNDS

Environmental impact estimates were made using the Environmental Paper Network Paper Calculator 3.2. For more information visit www.papercalculator.org.